About The Author

Kamiya Nicole is a wife, mother, entrepreneur, and mentor. Her love for fashion, hair and beauty led her to launch Kamiya Nicole Enterprises LLC in 2016.

Her online store caters to women's fashion needs which includes apparel, accessories, custom apparel & items and hair extensions.

Still learning and thriving, she created this planner to help like minded people to reach their fullest potential and live the life God intended for them to live.

WHO'S THIS PLANNER FOR?

This planner was created with you in mind.
Sometimes we just need to sit down and write down our vision, make it plain, and execute.
This planner provides you with calendars, daily affirmations, notes pages, and goals trackers to help you reach your potential.

Get ready, Get set, Go!

IT BELONGS TO ME

supernatural grace
supernatural favor
supernatural strength
supernatural overflow
supernatural increase
supernatural wisdom
supernatural discernment
supernatural endurance
supernatural peace
supernatural abundance
supernatural joy
supernatural sustainment
supernatural obedience
supernatural zeal
supernatural wealth
supernatural growth
supernatural excellence
supernatural freedom

DAILY AFFIRMATIONS

1. I am Strong. I am ready. I am willing. I am determined.
2. I constantly attract opportunities that create wealth, peace and favor.
3. I have the freedom and the power to create the life that God intended for me to live and the life that I desire.
4. I am determined to succeed and accomplish the goals I have set for myself.
5. I am surrounded by the love of Christ and his love has set me free of hurt, pain, and sorrow.
6. I walk in power, with strength and authority
7. I am who God called me to be and I am not afraid to be who he wants me to be.
8. I accept my failures as they are only stepping stones to prevail in my future.

JANUARY

date: ______________________________

notes:

sun	mon	tue	wed	thu	fri	sat

JANUARY

GOALS FOR THE MONTH

- [ ]
- [ ]
- [ ]
- [ ]
- [ ]
- [ ]

DATES TO REMEMBER

IMPORTANT NOTES

- [ ]
- [ ]
- [ ]
- [ ]
- [ ]
- [ ]
- [ ]
- [ ]
- [ ]
- [ ]
- [ ]
- [ ]

MY NOTES

MY NOTES

FEBRUARY

date: ______________________

notes:

sun	mon	tue	wed	thu	fri	sat

FEBRUARY

GOALS FOR THE MONTH

- [ ] ______
- [ ] ______
- [ ] ______
- [ ] ______
- [ ] ______
- [ ] ______

DATES TO REMEMBER

IMPORTANT NOTES

- [ ] ______
- [ ] ______
- [ ] ______
- [ ] ______
- [ ] ______
- [ ] ______
- [ ] ______
- [ ] ______
- [ ] ______
- [ ] ______
- [ ] ______
- [ ] ______

MY NOTES

MY NOTES

MARCH

date: ______________________

notes:

sun	*mon*	*tue*	*wed*	*thu*	*fri*	*sat*

MARCH

GOALS FOR THE MONTH

- [ ] ______________________________
- [ ] ______________________________
- [ ] ______________________________
- [ ] ______________________________
- [ ] ______________________________
- [ ] ______________________________

DATES TO REMEMBER

IMPORTANT NOTES

- [ ] ______________________________
- [ ] ______________________________
- [ ] ______________________________
- [ ] ______________________________
- [ ] ______________________________
- [ ] ______________________________
- [ ] ______________________________
- [ ] ______________________________
- [ ] ______________________________
- [ ] ______________________________
- [ ] ______________________________
- [ ] ______________________________

MY NOTES

MY NOTES

APRIL

date: ______________________

notes:

sun	mon	tue	wed	thu	fri	sat

APRIL

GOALS FOR THE MONTH

- [ ] ______
- [ ] ______
- [ ] ______
- [ ] ______
- [ ] ______
- [ ] ______

DATES TO REMEMBER

IMPORTANT NOTES

- [ ] ______
- [ ] ______
- [ ] ______
- [ ] ______
- [ ] ______
- [ ] ______
- [ ] ______
- [ ] ______
- [ ] ______
- [ ] ______
- [ ] ______
- [ ] ______

MY NOTES

MY NOTES

MAY

date: ____________________

notes:

sun	mon	tue	wed	thu	fri	sat

MAY

GOALS FOR THE MONTH

- [ ]
- [ ]
- [ ]
- [ ]
- [ ]
- [ ]

DATES TO REMEMBER

IMPORTANT NOTES

- [ ]
- [ ]
- [ ]
- [ ]
- [ ]
- [ ]
- [ ]
- [ ]
- [ ]
- [ ]
- [ ]
- [ ]

MY NOTES

MY NOTES

JUNE

date: ______________________

notes:

sun	mon	tue	wed	thu	fri	sat

JUNE

GOALS FOR THE MONTH

- [ ] ______
- [ ] ______
- [ ] ______
- [ ] ______
- [ ] ______
- [ ] ______

DATES TO REMEMBER

IMPORTANT NOTES

- [ ] ______
- [ ] ______
- [ ] ______
- [ ] ______
- [ ] ______
- [ ] ______
- [ ] ______
- [ ] ______
- [ ] ______
- [ ] ______
- [ ] ______
- [ ] ______

MY NOTES

MY NOTES

JULY

date: ______________________

notes:

sun	mon	tue	wed	thu	fri	sat

JULY

GOALS FOR THE MONTH

- [ ]
- [ ]
- [ ]
- [ ]
- [ ]
- [ ]

DATES TO REMEMBER

IMPORTANT NOTES

- [ ]
- [ ]
- [ ]
- [ ]
- [ ]
- [ ]
- [ ]
- [ ]
- [ ]
- [ ]
- [ ]
- [ ]

MY NOTES

MY NOTES

AUGUST

date: ____________________

notes:

sun	mon	tue	wed	thu	fri	sat

AUGUST

GOALS FOR THE MONTH

- [ ] ____
- [ ] ____
- [ ] ____
- [ ] ____
- [ ] ____
- [ ] ____

DATES TO REMEMBER

IMPORTANT NOTES

- [ ] ____
- [ ] ____
- [ ] ____
- [ ] ____
- [ ] ____
- [ ] ____
- [ ] ____
- [ ] ____
- [ ] ____
- [ ] ____
- [ ] ____
- [ ] ____

MY NOTES

MY NOTES

SEPTEMBER

date: ______________________

notes:

sun	mon	tue	wed	thu	fri	sat

SEPTEMBER

GOALS FOR THE MONTH

- [ ] ______
- [ ] ______
- [ ] ______
- [ ] ______
- [ ] ______
- [ ] ______

DATES TO REMEMBER

IMPORTANT NOTES

- [ ] ______
- [ ] ______
- [ ] ______
- [ ] ______
- [ ] ______
- [ ] ______
- [ ] ______
- [ ] ______
- [ ] ______
- [ ] ______
- [ ] ______
- [ ] ______

MY NOTES

MY NOTES

OCTOBER

date: ____________________

notes:

sun	mon	tue	wed	thu	fri	sat

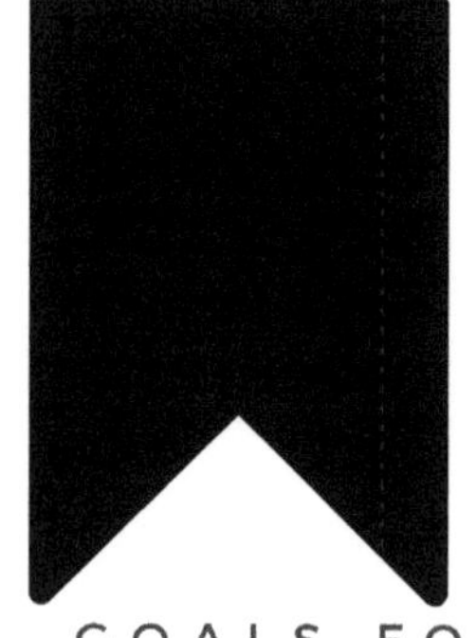

OCTOBER

GOALS FOR THE MONTH

- [ ]
- [ ]
- [ ]
- [ ]
- [ ]
- [ ]

DATES TO REMEMBER

IMPORTANT NOTES

- [ ]
- [ ]
- [ ]
- [ ]
- [ ]
- [ ]
- [ ]
- [ ]
- [ ]
- [ ]
- [ ]
- [ ]

MY NOTES

MY NOTES

NOVEMBER

date: ______________________

notes:

sun	mon	tue	wed	thu	fri	sat

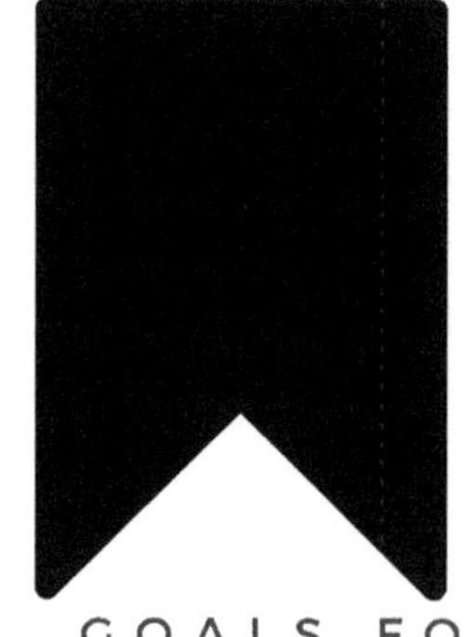

NOVEMBER

GOALS FOR THE MONTH

- [ ] ______
- [ ] ______
- [ ] ______
- [ ] ______
- [ ] ______
- [ ] ______

DATES TO REMEMBER

IMPORTANT NOTES

- [ ] ______
- [ ] ______
- [ ] ______
- [ ] ______
- [ ] ______
- [ ] ______
- [ ] ______
- [ ] ______
- [ ] ______
- [ ] ______
- [ ] ______
- [ ] ______

MY NOTES

MY NOTES

DECEMBER

date: ______________________

notes:

sun	mon	tue	wed	thu	fri	sat

DECEMBER

GOALS FOR THE MONTH

- [ ]
- [ ]
- [ ]
- [ ]
- [ ]
- [ ]

DATES TO REMEMBER

IMPORTANT NOTES

- [ ]
- [ ]
- [ ]
- [ ]
- [ ]
- [ ]
- [ ]
- [ ]
- [ ]
- [ ]
- [ ]
- [ ]

MY NOTES

MY NOTES

IAmKamiyaNicole.com

9 780557 990337

www.ingramcontent.com/pod-product-compliance
Ingram Content Group UK Ltd.
Pitfield, Milton Keynes, MK11 3LW, UK
UKHW050148280726
14058UKWH00007B/888